Empty
like a Pocket

I0080150

Molly McDonald

Up On Big Rock Poetry Series
SHIPWRECKT BOOKS PUBLISHING COMPANY

IN®
DIE

Cover photo by Adam Kindred
Cover by Shipwreckt Books

Contents

The raveling, the unraveling, the body, the blood, the spirit, the nougat, the marrow, the core, the pit, the illusion, the crossroads, the cake and its consumption without considering the baker or the indigestion, the life, the suffering, the middle or when what happens, happens.

The End

Tuxedo

It feels like just yesterday I was supposed to get married
I was supposed to get married yesterday
Today I took a shower in my tuxedo
I've been spilling a lot of ice cream on myself in the last
24 hours
I'm sorry that I was in your shower when you woke up
I wanted to bring you some ice cream
I wanted to scream and scream at you
Until the ice in your eyes melted
I forgot how hard it is to get wax out of fabric
I've been lighting a lot of candles lately
Or just since yesterday afternoon
I was standing at the altar for so long
My legs got tired
It got dark and the stained glass windows
Died
I lit candle after candle to see
stay warm
let the wax run down my arms
To make sure I could still feel something
It didn't work
But I'm pretty sure
I'm not going to get this
Tuxedo deposit
Returned
I might as well wear it
To my funeral

Sno Cone

I knew a stripper with attention deficit disorder. She'd
trade her meds for tattoos to cover up her track marks.
She'd change her hair like some folks change their
underwear

every week whether it needs it or not. Mama said keep
it clean in case of an accident. I guess that's what you
could call it. I guess she was someone's daughter

harder to picture than the mistress scenario. Drinking
rum like it was closer to water and handing over
compliments like they were someone

else's credit card. Driving cars, breaking hearts, telling
lies like it was an art form perfected instead of
addiction's twisted fiction. Dripping venom like puppet
strings that tell you to eat

eat, eat. Sticky like candy and sweet like disease. Watch
those lips move, you can barely see the strings.
Listen closely

you can hardly hear a heart beat. You can't even hear a
heart beat.

SchadenFreud

When dreams die do they shrivel up or explode or fall over or erode slowly or get buried alive and suffocate, eyes wide with terror? Sometimes a cigar is just a cigar and sometimes it's the spark you need to light a fuse that will take you so much further. Sometimes love is the answer but sometimes it asks too many questions so you have to duct tape its mouth shut and throw it on the trash heap with the rest of your expired dreams.

Swum

Heartbreak isn't hearts broken as much as tongues crossed, frozen, then pulled off the metal bars on each other's jungle gym. What you've lost is always more than what you're left with. Fewer taste buds means the world is less delicious. More treacherous in the open ocean with wounds bleeding.

Yesterday, we were swimming in each other.

Now I'm just watching the sharks circle my ankles while you shiver on the sea shore. She sells spells that would help this.

She gives them away. She's gone away.

Taking my skin with her.

Kafka esque

I burned my tongue on all your promises now I can't
taste any of the words you say. Even though you're far
away, each time I hear your name my teeth break but
my bones stay strong from all the milk I've drowned
my sorrows in.
Turns out sorrow can swim.
Turns out I'm lactose intolerant. My coping
mechanisms are torture devices. Everything I do seems
backward. Maybe I should stop looking in the mirror
but in the right light my tears reflected shine like
diamonds. Like I closed my eyes so tight on all the coal
from my stocking and overnight, metamorphosis. I'm
still more beetle than human but I'm working on
keeping up appearances. Santa sees me when I'm
sleeping but I'm not even here, then. I'm burrowed so
far inside my head I found a China that no one knows
about. There are clouds of soot and time has slowed to
a crawl so I don't get stepped on even when I'm
flipped on my back. I'm hopelessly out of whack and
black and blue but that's nothing new or different. My
feelers are numb from butting up against the memory
of us.
Like a great wall, it is.
Like a whole other country. I lost my passport and wish
I could say the same of the maps we traced with our
feet and the choruses we wrote together. When I wake
up, I try to stretch all six of my legs and come up short.
It takes hours to sort myself out and by then it's time to
lie down again. I'm no entomologist but I think I'm
crazy. I'm no doctor but I wish you'd stop bugging me.
I know you're not here but you're not leaving, either.

ThinBlueLine

Microscopic looming everything. The power of positive
and the negative thinking it shits through holes like a
shower head. Bang bang, you're dead. Ready or not hot
or cold over easy I'm over it this is too easy I'm
freezing I'm frozen it's done. Empty oven and all the
chickens flew away while I was gone. I do all my own
tricks but it stunted my growth. I write all my own
jokes but they sound wrong in my throat. My stomach
is upside down and I think I'll hide forever. You know
the Nazis had bruises they made the Jews wear. Still are.
Make art or fall apart or World War or lay down your
swords or spit or swallow or follow this red river out of
here or wallow in the salt water womb and I'll think
about you when I taste my tears.

Movie Plot

This curse is a blessing
This blessing is a curse
All I want
Is what I had
All along

Cliff Hanger

Like a herd of buffalo I heard the thunder of running
and dust plumes like blood blooms wet and modest in
the cautious grass precipice. To fall further meant dirt
and under that and under that. Forgotten and bought
and sold and traded for old hats and new beaded
beginnings. Slick like birthday suits taut across saw
bones. I saw horses. And a moon on the horizon like
the wide open mouth of evening. I fell like something
ephemeral and choreographed. In a past life I was
disfigured and broken. Before that something wild with
hooves. Even earlier were feathers and spiral diving.

Birds dropping from the air. What a thought. What a
feeling.

Eulogy

I played a round of golf to raise money for your
surgery and I bought you all the tissues you needed to
cry into. And then some. I still find boxes tucked in
closets and crinkly wads behind the head board. What
more do you want from me?

I'll bring flowers to your grave site and light a candle
in your memory. I'd put your picture in the living
room but you're not any more so I'll hang it on
the fridge like a failed report card.

On our anniversary, I'll wear a black shirt and eat at a
restaurant we've never been to and refuse to smile at
the waitress. I'll eat half of everything and forget to tip
and then drive around faster than the speed limit on
black topped back roads known for their lack of cop
cars and abundance of beer cans. I'll drink too much
and pass out in an arm chair and show up late for work
the next day and dare them to fire me.

I will ooze grief like pus from an infected wound and
accept condolences and casseroles from your family
but I don't know if I'll eat them. Your mother was
always such a bad cook. You had that in common.

Baby Steps

In a car crash there are 3 collisions

1) Your car with the brick wall
2) Your body with the steering wheel
3) Your organs with your ribcage

Two and three can change depending on where you are in the vehicle. Sometimes

2) is your baby's head with the windshield and

3) is her small brain - the tiny lobes that make her smile and kick and almost say mama - with her fragile skull There are 7 stages of grieving but having the cliffs notes in front of you doesn't make it any easier. Telling yourself that you're

in shock but will soon feel guilty and then

angry and then depressed and then

it will get better is not helpful

Better is a word that can only matter in context and in the context of a black hole, everything is shades of complete darkness. When you gave birth to her, you didn't want an epidural. Wanted to feel the whole thing while it happened because you knew it would be worth the pain and the pain would be a voucher of suffering that you would exchange for years and years of motherhood.

Right now you just want to be numb, numbed,

dumbed down till what's happening is so beyond your comprehension that you retreat to your animal brain and stop trying to understand.

Elephants grieve for their dead children and bury them under leaves and sticks. Ears droop and eyes sink back into the skin of their face till they are like buttons on a leather couch. Crows can recognize faces and even pass this knowledge on to their young. They are also distracted by shiny things. Red and blue lights and this siren that is coming from outside and inside your head and now you can't imagine life without it.

Reflections

There was a girl who thought every mirror was a window. She was stalked by someone beautiful and unknowable. Every pool of water was a portal to a shimmery world. Her microwave was a buzzing box that fit exactly one head.

There was a man who thought every window was a mirror. He was a god alternately in awe with and disgusted by the world he embodied.

There was a girl who drowned, her brain buzzing with anticipation while it was starved of oxygen.

There was a man who moved into a Salt Lake City apartment that faced a wall of Tetris symmetry. He became a god of bricks and a god of straight cement lines and he saw it and it wasn't just good, it was good enough.

Slippery Sunset

The beginning was full of whimpers and bangs like a starter gun, like frightened dogs, like electric shocks from your mother's hair dryer used as a microphone when the phone rang, when the door slammed.

When the delivery man and your mother slowly took off each other's clothes in the next room and didn't make a sound.

It was the sudden silence that made your fingers so slippery and the hair dryer met a wet end in the bathtub. Electric like a sunset, you ended with whimpers like slippers across wood floors and the bang of your head against porcelain.

Sepia

In the summer you place tea bags in a glass jar with water and bring it to the back porch. You hardly come out here anymore even though it gets the best sun.

You don't wipe away the dust as you set the jar on an end table next to a notebook filled with verb conjugations. Stuffy rooms bother your sinuses.

Underneath the notebook is a Bible nailed shut and filled with family secrets. Life sentences. The words that make up your existence. The whole room is an Olympic sized swimming pool in the off season. A mass grave. A warehouse filled with slightly irregular greeting cards. This room gets the best sun so you're expecting results. Who doesn't love tea in the summertime?

In the winter you wait until the streets are cleared to drive to the store. In the empty parking lot you carefully adjust the handicapped sign hanging from the rear view mirror and walk toward the entrance. Cold air bothers your sinuses. The doors open themselves and you're greeted by a chilled tower of butter substitutes. There is no ocean of sound. The speaker system must be broken. The store is like an Olympic sized swimming pool in the off season. You swim through the aisles, forgetting what you came for. You settle for a carton of lemonade, wishing you'd lived your life differently.

All My Friends

All my friends are failing their drug tests
Sleeping in the mess of the beds they've made
And dreaming of sleeping some more
All off my friends are slamming doors
Or letting them hang open
Their pets are escaping
Cats let out of bags lick up spilled milk
And we've all forgotten how to cry
All of my friends are high
But could be higher
Blood thinned
By fire and water
So you could swim in it
Or drown
All of my friends are just hanging out
Or staying in
All of my friends are confessing their sins
And their sins are so silly
All my friends are OD'ing
It's a bummer, my dad says
And it is
It really is.

Swamp Song

It was the west of times. It was the burst of times. Directional hemorrhage. Splits in the beams and the rafters falling after before I knew you. Before your lips carved my ear out of marble and I was sculpted and perfected and forgotten. Shatter skulls and bone on bone in tombs in gloomy stadiums. Whose limb where now? What embraces we collapse into. What shapes we make with our defeated eyes and fingers.

It was a cursed time. It was a nest of sharp rocks and the ocean pounded like a heart and sighed like something dying slowly. All the bugs in our intestines converged on a battlefield and immediately gave up. It was hopelessly over and the flags burned and the churning masses made cream then butter and melted away toward the sunset on the western horizon.

Apology

Plaster casted Praying Mantis
I beg forgiveness
I had no business
Reaching up into the rafters
I bumped your body
And it shattered

Bosnian Haircut

Bang, Bangs! Now I can't see. Now Ow my eyes. How this hair grows like vines along church walls. Bang, Bangs! Now shrapnel in temples. Shrapnel in temples and the altar and the carpets all red, wet. Bad dogma! Go outside and preach to the masses on the hillside.

Guided by the highest of voices, the lightest of stars. Ask yourself the questions you ask of others. You think you can, you think you can, and so you am. And so am

I. And yet the why still dangles in front of my eyes like tangles of hair and ignorance. Bangs, Bang! And cover your ears and hear no evil. And. And love. And love one. And love one another. And another and another one. And then it ended with whimper.

Bus Fuck

I feel it would help the reader to know that this was written as a reaction to the gang rape and subsequent death of a woman on a bus in Delhi, India in 2012.

Oh god. Fuck. I can't believe we're... Shit. Shit. Shh, it's late and your voice is hot like diesel fumes spiderwebbing through decomposing streets.

Wha... what?

Cut, release, cleaved like continents. Tension, pull, burst from the earth, carrots from dirt. Dangled. Lazy skirt. Scream. The clean light of day breaking, emerald,   ruby slipped her a mickey now her tongue's all sticky to the roof of my mouth. You can see the stars from here, the city. Pity you're not awake for this, slut. Must need your sleep, eyes rolled back slack jawed attack dogs stopped firing when the electricity went out. Rock beats sister cuts phone cord drywall coats my shoulders head through walls and space and time.

Apology. Silence as Acceptance.

Take off your pants like everyone. Seed. Spell. Sick. Charming. Charming insistence like razor blade chocolates. So white my head is melting. Blue. Orange. Banana. I mean yellow. Brick roads and wood houses. Splinters. Couch cushions so far from home I couldn't eat another bite I'm stuffed. Cunt. Give thanks. Take this all of you and fucking eat it you'll eat it all oh it's so good you like it don't you? You can't get enough.

Whore. Virgin. Mother Theresa. Black on the inside but only because there's no light. We'll have to cut her open with diamonds. With our quick, blind tongues. What we find might surprise us but the signs were there all along.

Thumbs fumbling under seats. Ripping seams. Miss stiches. Match strike lighting flick zippo cigarette. No smoking, please sir I ask you please very nice this is a clean place no smoking sir.

Please. Dis ease.

Creased thigh. Eye of the needle it will be harder for you to fit through than... Finger fucking point made in a ring around the rows, eyes like empty pockets. No woman, no cry little piggy. We, we, we. And us. Blown away. Washed out. Rainspout. Waterslide. Down the throats and out the eyes. Round stones of bone carved with an X and traded for room and board and I'm bored and boring holes in my mind filled with nothing but silence on the border of obscene what I've seen erases everything I haven't. Black board horror stories keep your opals and rubies they're just rocks and I'm so far above this and you're so far inside me and we're all hiding in plain sight.

Seek. What will my mother

think? And where will she put my ashes? Ashes.

Awful. All fall. Done.

The raveling, the unraveling, the body, the blood, the spirit, the nougat, the marrow, the core, the pit, the illusion, the crossroads, the cake and its consumption without considering the baker or the indigestion, the life, the suffering, the middle or when what happens, happens.

Tuxedo II

I wrote you from Antarctica.

On a postcard everything's a poem.

Dear You,

My eyelashes have frozen and fallen off.

The world is all black and white like Stevie Wonder and Wonder bread. Sometimes I wonder if I'm dead then I cough and my breath

forms a cloud in front of me like a swarm of bees,

freezing and falling, shattering on the South Pole like

wine glasses in a hurricane.

From,

Me

You never write back or maybe my

messenger penguin got lost,

died,

fell in love and forgot us both.

Peep Hole

People hurt people People heal people

People love, hate, fuck, fight, lie, cheat, steal, peel back the skin over each other's ribs and spit on the fragile muscle of a beating heart before walking away.

People lay down on beds of nails so that others may walk over them without ruining their shoes.

People lose more than they want but win more than they know.

People laugh, smile, hug, cry, cry, cry, smile, die eventually.

That's people for ya. People are poetry.

People learn from their mistakes and are so predictable it's ridiculous

I knew you were going to do that before you did, before I said what I said, before your mom knew your dad, and before we all crawled out of Africa.

People use words as tools and blunt objects as communication and when those don't work they bang their heads against brick walls or scream or give up or get back up or start a band.

People try and fail and fall and try and fail. And people are people.

Which is shitty and wonderful. But mostly just reality. Humanity's the most exclusive club that everyone belongs to, and we're constantly paying our dues.

Take me to Your Leader

Take me to your leader.

Feed her grapes and episodes of Futurama. Let her grow up so that she may see over the crowd at bus stops. Or, let her learn to stand on benches and tree stumps when she wants to be taller than she is.

Otherwise hidden like warm in winter. Quiet like a mime but always thinking. You can see it in her eyes. You can feel it when she's breathing. All ideas and possibility.

It's not the heat, it's the humanity. It's the heavy blankets of expectation in the middle of July. It's the boxes we build for other people to crawl into and die before we bury them but long after we've stopped paying attention. It's our own short sightedness. It's tragic ass-backwards assumptions that play out because we've already written them down. It's the cart before the horse, the carrot dangling from a noose in front of our nose. The bright invitingness of toy store windows. The biting off more than we can chew disease with making excuses symptoms. The way we are doomed to repeat history because we're running away from it so quickly. The frosting we spread on shit and celebrate like birthday cake. The way we cross our fingers when we blow out the candles because we don't trust the wishes we're making. Don't believe that we can really make anything happen besides stepping on toes and watching car crashes, slow motion destruction of the rain forest. Blinking and missing the happy ending. And the new beginning. And the sunrise. And your eyes.

And my eyes.

Dear fingertips, lead me to temptation. Dear brain, stop over thinking. Dear heart, stop under

standing. Dear feet, take me where you're going. Take me to your leader.

I'd really like to meet her.

Just behind your third eye, always laughing. Mine's doing the same but sometimes it's hard to hear unless you hold your breath and stop listening.

Cicada Jesus

Cicada Jesus sheds his skin like the hard plastic that electronics come in. Cicada Jesus sounds like dinosaurs and cellphones vibrating off of wooden tables. Cicada Jesus is pious like 3.14159 pizza time. No cheese please but all of the onions. Cicada Jesus is layers of meaning and nice-ing. He's never think twice-ing because there are too many things already.

Not really.

There are only a few things in different costumes. Cicada Jesus turns off the news and switches to cartoons instead. He likes the way the colors tickle his head. He knows that he is because he thinks but he won't imagine when he doesn't because he can't. He's not going to worry about it.

He's going to drink some coffee now.

Cicada Jesus's mug has a picture of the planet Earth. Coffee lava and coffee dirt. What kind of Band Aid works for hurt feelings? Cicada Jesus spends a lot of time thinking about this. Maybe Cicada Jesus will plant a tree today. Maybe he'll climb up halfway and cling to the bark like a shark to the ocean. Maybe he'll close his eyes because Cicada Jesus is tired and he still doesn't have a job but he'll start looking tomorrow. Cicada Jesus knows that there's always tomorrow. He checked his calendar. The kitten on the cover told him to hang in there. Cicada Jesus obeys and falls asleep to the sound of the radio through the window of a house where someone beautiful lives.

black

My Goth daughter is such a virgin. Such a dark version
of the world like underexposed photos like underwater
limbo ballroom dancing. My Goth daughter is corset,
batwing, mascara, I don't care about you thoughts and
my hypothesis is that I don't care either. You can build
something for 9 months and spit it out. You can grow it
in a house for 15 years and then watch it fall down
around your ears. I can't hear you, I say. And she
mumbles again. Or growls. Or she's suffocating. Maybe
she'll die right here. Maybe she'd like that. My Goth
daughter is so boring it's like she's gone all ready. My
Goth daughter is such a whore, is such a Halloween
novelty she's like candy. But not sweet at all. Like a
cardboard cupcake filled with sand and hate.

Mess Age

Like an inky ocean slapping stained glass shores. Like
an octopus exploded on linoleum floors. Hieroglyphic
sunsets tell the future like, it's going to be dark soon.
Let the moon do the photocopying while you watch the
stars burn through the sky like cigarettes on bed sheets,
ashy constellations. The pictures in my head bleed out
my eyes and into yours. Heart beat as Morse code.
Breathing sounds like the ocean waving semaphore.
Secret codes in four languages get distorted when you're
speaking under water. Echoes are cave's way of being
louder than they are. Sinus headache take two of these
call me every day rain or sunshine show me yours I'll
see if I can find mine under this pile of birth certificates.
Nostalgia is sepia. Piss stained bedsheets.
We're doomed to repeat, wet the bed over and over
again. Good thing I'm not afraid of it. I packed a lunch
and didn't make friends, get pets or plants in the first
place. I'm a blank page. I never started smoking so I've
got nothing to quit but I'll stop talking, sit quietly and
believe the pictures in your head

Truth or Consequences, NM

Form follows function deep into a canyon in a small car
that's built for parking lots, not camping. The tires puff
up dust that hovers lazy over chiseled cliffs like God's
dog gnawing on rock then bounding off, leaving raw
prints that fill with gritty rain water.
They become lost but not forgotten. Their hair gets wild
and mats together when they sleep close cold nights in
the desert. They separate themselves in the morning
with a lit cigarette then share it for breakfast. The smell
of burnt hair wears them like a suit jacket it doesn't
want to take off because there's nothing underneath. It's
an empty promise.
Form becomes reformed becomes Performance
becomes more style than substance like an antique
rotary phone, twirling twirling but no one home.
Function limps into dysfunction like a rosary made
from the baby teeth of pagan children and dropped into
the ocean. Drifts for a while. Lands on a coral reef
pretty like a sunset, like silent disappointment.
Performance and Dysfunction share one last cigarette
before they part ways forever. One never smokes again
and the other switches to cigars. One dies quietly at
night, looking at the stars fenced in by the buzzing of
insects. The other starts the car on the first try. Drives
with headlights safety pinned to the rocks ahead and
loose gravel spitting encouragement.
Civilization is just how they left it, like a pair of pajamas
too small and faded.

Capital T Truth

One time I synced up a bunch of sunscreen commercials to a Stairway to Heaven soundtrack and for eight minutes life made so much sense that I laughed and milk squirted out of my nose. But I hadn't been drinking milk so life didn't make sense anymore and I wondered if it ever really had.

This way, to the see

'I don't want you to see me this way' sounds like
something you would say without thinking.
I don't want you to think that this is the way it sounds.
Without thinking, I want you to see the way I sound.
You are something that thinks the sounds I want to like.
You want to see, say, think without me this way.
This way sounds like something you don't want.
Don't you think that this is something I would say?
Thinking this, I don't want, only see.
Sound is you and me this way.
Something you want.
Me thinking Want something.
You me You.
I think like this.
I want you to see me.
Yes, she is pretty, isn't she?

Dangling Conversations

I.

How's your ex-wife? she asked.

All right, I answered, she caught a fish the other day.

By being such a crazy bitch? she asked.

No, I said, just the usual way.

That's so like her, she scoffed.

Really? I said. It surprised the hell out of me.

II.

All my sisters are nuns. She said.

None of my brothers are boy scouts. You said. But they can sure tie knots.

You show her the raw strips on your wrists where rope has rubbed back and forth and pulled the skin with it.

She hikes up the back of her shirt so you can see the melted pucker design over her ribs.

Holy water. She says.

Jesus Christ. You say.

She flinches.

III.

What's that song you're singing? She asks.

I'm not singing. You say.

What were you humming, then? She asks.

Not humming. You answer.

What are you doing over there? She asks.

Praying. You say.

Praying for what? She asks.

For a song. You say. A song to strike down like lighting through my skull and out my lips and burn the ears of whomever hears it with joy so hot it feels like dying and being born at the same time.

It sounded like 'Under the Sea.' she says

That makes sense. You say. I was praying to the Little Mermaid.

IV.

What are these beautiful tapestries? She asked. Silk?

Those are my emotions! I yelled. And they're felt.

She was floored. I was linoleum.

It's easier to wipe up spills. I said.

Genius! She said. But I'm more rugged. I like to feel the crumbs in my pile.

You're a pile! I yelled.

Oh I get it. She said. Poop joke.

You're a joke! I yelled.

And she laughed. But

I didn't get it.

Omelet

I was gonna make my bed but I made a joke instead.
And I cracked myself up like I was made of a million
eggs. I laughed a whole symphony like my organs were a
horn section. I was born again in comedy cause god's a
silly bastard. I danced without pants cause it's hot in my
apartment. I got tangled up in blankets cause I didn't
make my bed today. I hit my head, lost my memory. It's
pretty sad cause I was gonna tell you my joke but I got
brain damage instead.

Somnambulist

I used to run laps around the neighborhood in my sleep until I started smoking.

Then I started sleep walking. Pretty soon I was sleep wheezing, leaning over with my hands on my knees, spitting ropes of phlegm into the neighbor's lawn.

Eventually, it became easier to blow smoke out the window as I sleep drove to the gas station, got a cup of coffee and told the cashier about my problems. The coffee would wake me up mid-anecdote and my brain would feel muddled and unsure of itself until I stepped outside for a cigarette.

I felt like I was cheating myself because I'd heard that the first of the day is the best and I always smoked it in my sleep. As the glow from my second bled into the sky to become the light of morning, I'd wander back inside. "I've got problems," I'd say to the guy behind the counter.

"I know." He'd answer, "You already told me."

Frumious Bandersnatch

I know you don't need all your skin. Let me make a lampshade so the light shines through when I write you letters on paper from trees shedding leaves leaving home.

I know those colors aren't yours. But can we share? Is it apparent I'm a parrot marionette? Mouthing words I learned from listening at thin walls then flying away?

Feather mirage. Garage door. Hardcore iron ore diamond in the rough tongue. Cat eyes. Real lies. Realize. Relay the impulse from my brain to my training bra. Trampoline religion.

Let me twirl and twirl like Jewish tradition. Like Hurricane Alphabet soup. Empty eyes washed up on the beach. It's dark now and I can see the stars but I wish on my toes that they take me where I want to go and that I keep on following. That they tell me what I should know and I don't stop believing.

And that's just a Journey song but the journey is long and my pockets are full of quarters and the jukebox talks to me in verses how to go about my business so I flip the sign to open and dance like destruction herself was creating a new universe.

Escape hatch, 80 proof

Star light, moon shine. Sun bites hard on my eyes while my throat swallows liquid dynamite. Burning guts and spinning sky. There are two of you and not enough of me. I am a picnic basket short of a picnic basket, just holding all these sandwiches in my lap. How romantic. Slapping pieces of bread together with one hand and clapping with the other. Someone forgot the applause. Someone forgot the apple sauce. Someone didn't forget, they just lost their mind and they're going to find it. And they're going to be right back. They promise. They swear on the light from the stars and front of cars and candles on fire in churches.

Fun House

The cave of my consciousness is cool and dark like an amusement park after midnight in the off season. I do my best overthinking in here. Most understanding.

Sitting cross legged makes my feet go to sleep and once I'm at peace with the numbness I tell my lap about my problems. I wear corduroy pants and as they dance up and down they scratch out the sound of a fire trying to start, a heart pumping nails, a piñata full of hail and marbles falling bouncing on a wood floor.

That's no kind of answer but it passes for conversation in these parts.

The art of being alone is delicate and heavy. It's eyes that are shut but see everything. It's stillness and feeling filled up with meaning. It's draining worry like pus from an infection and welcoming the maggots into your ecosystem. It's turning into something bigger and winged after breaking out of your old skin. It's swallowing whole your ugliness and not asking for seconds. Content with time stretching as far as you can see in both directions and meeting up like a Mobius strip or roller coaster track cracked and abandoned after midnight in January.

BCE

Ouch! Feelings.

What if, like tree, we put bark on legs so skin safe? So squirrels can still live, we put pockets.

Is that squirrel in yours or just excited with penis that I here?

Karl

His name is Karl. His hair sticks to his forehead like spaghetti noodles fused to the kitchen wall. You know the way marinara bubbles down the side of the pan to sizzle on the burner? I think about that when Karl shows me the places that he's cut himself. Ouch I think. Yum.

Christmas Story

My dumb numb fingers bumble buttons through holes
and grip zippers like they were crucifixes. The trick to
this is to stop thinking and let your muscles move
smoothly like a spoon through pudding or pus from a
wound, a damsel swooning in slow motion from the
sight of blood blooming in a bouquet of stigmata. I've
got a secret garden that God forgot about. It's behind
the library and you can sit for eternity watching letters
grow into words and tangle together till they're Bible
verses. The Christ child laughs like one hundred stars
shattering. Away in a manger and in danger of
becoming strung up on a cross like Christmas lights
from the gutters where icicles hover waiting to poke
your eye out.

Optimist Prime

Don't pee on my parade and say it's my birthday. Don't blow out my candles and tell me it's windy. Don't set my trousers aflame and claim that I'm dishonest.

Don't tell me things are going to get better when I know that they're not.

Redemption Poem

Schrödinger said that novelty is all we pay attention to.
Everything else is auto pilot, muscle memory. Maybe it's
highs and lows we stumble on that make our lives
exciting. Maybe it's inevitable like a self-fulfilling
prophecy you saw in a dream once, I read in a book's
pages.

The mind decides and the body accepts it. The civil war
between what we want and what we know has so many
casualties. Nietzsche says that we become who

we are. Simon says lift your right arm and pat your left
cheek. Why are you hitting yourself? Why are you
hitting yourself?

I stay silent but all the words I swallow poke holes in
my stomach, hollow out a nest of regret to wallow in.
Sometimes grand gestures are just quiet funerals backlit
with expectations that explode like fireworks.

We see what we think we deserve and when reality falls
short we retreat into our own head and jimmy with the
circuitry. Solder excuses and sew together apologies.

The truth is better than any safety blanket but the truth
is always changing. Darwin says evolving. Einstein says
it's all relative. Marley says it'll be all right.

It'll be all right.

Hello Goodbye

As soon as I say adieu, I do, I do miss you.

I chew, achoo, oh no! Something's stuck in my windpipe! Come save me.

I'm blue. I blew it out, never mind. False alarm. Wait, you should still come back.

I miss, I miss you. Like the Inuit miss their igloo in racist cartoonland. We have so many words for snow! I snow shoe! I blow glue through a straw now I'm all ewwwww, wipe it off.

Spit Out

I've been licked by the long tongue of the law and mine is tied so I am silent and it's my right though it feels wrong to not speak up when I'm beat down and out in back alleys, ashtrays of the city.

Cat piss and misery and Yesterday is the song I'm singing while beetles scurry through invisible concrete fissures like a magic trick.

My hands are where they can see them and up my sleeves are bare arms and hatch marks measuring the days gone bye.

Today is the first day of the rest of my life sentence punctuated by sitting on the toilet and daydreams about slitting my wrists so vivid I have to kick myself to make sure I'm awake and alive and alone and untied and just as free as I was to begin with.

Chop

I played chopsticks until my mom slapped my hands. My dad just looked up and to the right like he wasn't there. He was floating above the room, detached and oblivious.

"They don't come to our restaurants and play forks!" mom hissed. She unrolled her fortune from the origami cookie and read it silently.

"They don't come to our restaurants and expect us to tell them their future," I whispered back and returned my fingers to the piano that was in the middle of the Chinese restaurant.

Or, as they call them, restaurants.

Negative Space

I'm not smart as much as dumb lucky. I'm not pretty as much as not ugly. I'm not awake as much as not sleeping and the dreams I'm having are bleeding into my belief system.

Sometimes I think I can fly. Sometimes I try. Sometimes I lie to myself about why I am, what I do, where I be, and what that means. Sometimes I believe what I think but usually I'm skeptical, like the times I know I'm invincible until a switch flips in my brain and I wish I was invisible, my fingerprints and the shadow I leave tainting the whole world like dirt in a laboratory. My whole life becomes an experiment, a test I'm failing. I'm too crazy.

I'm not crazy enough.

My consciousness expands and my muscles atrophy. My vocal cords are seized by this freezing up disease and the phone lines are disconnected. I'm ex-communicated. When I try to tell you what I mean my tongue gets tangled, I mix my metaphors, I shine light at odd angles and the font I'm using looks like another language. If this is what talking's for I'll take a vow of silence so I can only hurt myself with the words I'm not saying.

I'm not saying nothing as much as not not saying everything. I'm not dreaming as much as escaping. I'm not ugly as much as not existing. I'm not lucky as much as smart enough to quit before I even begin.

Make like a banana

I'll be fine as soon as I pay my debts to society and I
won't mind if I don't have to think about it and it's not
a crime if they don't catch me

and I'm always on time if I throw all my clocks away
and I'll keep watch if there's something to see

and I'll keep off the lawn if I learn how to read and I'll
follow the signs if they lead to the end and I'll start up
my car if you need a ride

and I'll find a dark hole if you ask me to hide and I'll
peel off my skin if it gets too hot

and I'll peel off my skin if you want

if you want.

Inside Joke

It's hard to find corners when you're looking for loopholes. Escape routes. Sticking to the edges of rooms and the rivers through forests with their banks worn down like patience, ego, identity. Worn down gently.

'It's hard to keep things straight without a jacket these days,' I say to the me in my head. She laughs. And laughs.

If you ever get lost in a corn field, find one row and follow it to the end. You'll emerge covered with whip-like slits all over your skin. You'll have broken through to the other side. Don't be let down when the view is pretty much the same. You can't tame everything.

Nothing is containable. Unless your container is large enough. See the whole world as your cauldron.

Remember when you tried to escape yourself by drinking an ocean of forgetfulness and woke up, your bed a raft on a sea of piss? Urine is sterile. You can drink it. If it comes to that, you can use my cup.

I want nothing but to give things away and empty myself. Thoughts and memories are porous like cheese cloth. When I walk, I pick up pieces of the road and shed skin, sweat, the tail end of whatever I'm humming at the moment.

How do we keep ourselves so separate? Is it skin? Fingerprints? The chemicals in my head tell me to throw myself, eyes first, at people on the street. Look through windows. Without my glasses, I can't see my own toes. Without the answers, I'm just as hopeless as everyone else. Which is a good place to start. Maybe we should start by looking under there. Under where?

Exactly.

Shape Shifting

Circle, spiral, line. Shapes dance behind my eyes but I need 3 dimensions to hide in. I need hard edges to climb but I'm afraid of heights. But I'm afraid I might like them. I'm a kite in a thunder storm in a story my mother told me and I'm electricity and I'm light and I'm light but I'm heavy. So I walk the tightrope while it lies on the ground. Like the horizon. Like the edges of my shadow which is who I was a second ago. Dark travels more slowly than light so she's always fighting to keep up.

Sometimes, at high noon and midnight, we stand nose to nose and look through each other's eyes. I see yesterday and she sees tomorrow. She always borrows and I pay it forward. We both owe each other everything so the slate's wiped clean. We're Even Steven, Adam and Eve in the Garden of Good and Evil. Heaven and Hell on a razor's edge like the difference between awake and dreaming but nothing is ever as its seeming so we have to believe in realness or suffer the consequences. Which are mostly flu like symptoms and a paper cutting of the soul. A red hot poker in the mind's eye and try as you might your skin is too tight for all of the yous you thought you were so blur the lines some more and before you know it you're back where you started like Dorothy waking up in Kansas or a rat racing backward through a maze of candy canes.

The circle of life. The spiral of time. The lines we cross but never finish and the walls we build to hide behind.

Color Wheel

I've read the darker the berry, the sweeter the fruit
I've let orange juice drip on my best suit
I yell 'oh, oh' through the window
Cause you marooned me here
With a green thumb but
No garden to grow
I blew up, saw red
Got violet and blacked out
I went toward the white light
Ended up over the rainbow
With some gold coins
I bought a joke book
What's black and white and red all over?
An Oreo with stigmata

Sauce, not Sauce

Sauces make me itchy. Sometimes I have to chant to myself 'It's a spread, it's a gravy. It's a potion, it's a lotion, it's a jelly' to keep from breaking out in hives. The mind is a powerful thing.

(A very small cross section of) Things I Like

Dr. Quinn: Medicine Woman, serendipity, improv comedy, heckling, complete silence, cast iron cookery, baby utensils, wearing kids' underwear, flossing, the way hydrogen peroxide fizzes, the periodic table, sautéing onions, not wearing pants, aprons, great apes, good escape stories, colloquialisms, wife beaters or whatever those tank tops are called, having a lot of quarters at my disposal, camping on the beach in Alaska, funny street signs, wide open spaces, niche friends, Sunkist orange soda, recycling, rock climbing, wearing pigtails, abandoned schools, night walking, podcasts, robes, Philip K. Dick and George Orwell, gender bending, breakdancing, roller skating, spitting, labor intensive foods like pistachios, unlocked doors, gas stoves, stream of consciousness, meta anything, cognitive dissonance, learning about biology, how the brain functions, nature or nurture, the way the fiddle is a violin, strip clubs, drinking holidays, camping supplies, beedis, the way that religion has emerged in almost every culture, the skin behind your ear under your arm and around your hipbones, snowstorms with lightning, eating just the filling out of pies, drunk philosophy talk with dads, sushi, wasabi, hot sauce, the smell of coriander, secret codes, wearing a watch, unfettered sneezes, eyelashes, Wikipedia, clipping coupons, squeegee-ing sweat off of eyebrows, picnics, finding dead cicadas, huge beanbags, compulsively checking the weather on the internet, protecting my hearing, headlamps!, packed lunches, five spice powder, Datsuns, driving stick shifts, the rush of adrenaline when you wake up late for work, front porches, baby rodents, calling hamsters 'hams,' thinking about pigs biting people, recreating the sound that I imagine this would create – as if people were made of crisp insulation, roasting chestnuts, eating with my hands, riding my bike through the woods at night with no lights, fireflies, hippos, not getting sunburned, overalls, hammers, succulents, the word somnambulism, caving, self-restraint, binge drinking, adults with braces, rocks shaped like states, lunchboxes, wrinkly hands, watch tan lines, bioregionalism, contextual realities, yarn, the sound made by hundreds of crows, shoveling snow, cutting other people's hair, pieces of flair, avocados,

jokes during oral sex, people who state the obvious, trailer courts, the way that snakes move, the way hair traps campfire smoke and lets it back out in the shower, writing love letters that don't make sense, defacing greeting cards, the Loch Ness monster, skeletons, accordions, Bahi'i temples, popcorn as a blank canvas, anthropomorphic fruits and vegetables, socks on wood floors, cats when you're tripping, funhouse mirrors, regional folk music, the original star trek, politically incorrect commercials, masturbating in public bathrooms, condiments, squatting, reflexology, seeing stars that have already burnt out, thinking about mortality, motor cycle rides, bike lanes, pick-up lines, kneading bread, opening jars, laugh lines, bars without televisions, jukeboxes, glass blowing, checking the weather report, cold cereal, guacamole, meditation, learning from experience, precocious children as long as they're far away from me, seeing babies dangling from a harness on their parent's torso, eskimo kisses, pronouncing aluminum like a Brit, sketch comedy, Heroin Bob from SLC Punk, Calvin and Hobbes, reading the Onion, comparing feet, standing on tiptoe, neck kisses, going to the chiropractor, showing instead of telling, hearing about other people's passive aggressiveness, making jokes about Ayn Rand, elaborate Halloween costumes, tree houses, rope ladders, jet skis, bonfires, youth hostels, hitchhiking, trapdoors, micro-lending, echoes, sitting in a tree and watching the day go by, peach cobbler, foot prints, the following description of a hangover: 'I didn't wake up as such – my disease just got this new open-eyed, standing up symptom.' Corduroy – cloth of the king! – soap that makes you tingle, symmetry, fractals, puddles, singing with pudding in your mouth, gargling hamsters, cushion forts, sleeping in station wagons, log cabins, the smell of maple syrup, laying on my belly in the grass, gangsta rap, sidewalk chalk, eating apples that are warm from being in the car, ham radios, walkie talkies, pez dispensers, butt cracks, watching people on the high dive, food stamps, crushing basil leaves, long underwear, running the wrong way up or down escalators, photo IDs, cookbooks with lots of pictures, slapping people's asses, people whom you always refer to using their first and last name, ethnobotany, whale sounds, giggling, pretending to have a penis, arguments over inconsequential things that let me know I've got PMS, friendly wait staff, flavored coffee, pantomiming drinking, boxes of wine, hydration, chimneys, crushed pennies, tiger lilies, photo booths, walking out of bad movies, clip on ties, mentally erasing the dog when I see people walking their pets with a bag of poop swinging from their hand, making grammatical errors for comedic effect, the music from Jurassic Park, negative pregnancy tests, genericized trademarks, Q-tips, Tetris, cracking my toes, chortling, ketchup on motherfucking everything, looking at the shelves full of mustard at the grocery store, festivals, chewed gum sculptures, deep inhales, cross country meets, the way that a mother peanut plant buries her own seeds, cabbage, toads, warm nights, streetlights next to flowers, illustrations in children's books, rodents, snakes, sewing, things in threes, pus, public transportation, the word 'curly,' surgeries, wristwatches, books about boarding schools, movies about misspent youth , math conversions in your head, blue and maroon, sideburns, soccer, cracking my toes, cleaning out sink drains, getting wet so I can get dry again, napping next to open windows, crossword puzzles, lighting things on fire, the smells of camping, laying on the ground looking skyward, trampolines, mosh pits, my own sweat, looking at maps, scars, metaphors, people falling down, nectarines, knives, bubble gum, carbonation, intoxication, euphoric hangovers, the multiple uses for bandanas, my mother swearing, being naked, having pockets, playlists, climbing trees, jazz hands, telling it like it is, arguments, fist fights, hugs, fingerprints, brain chemistry, trajectory, spider webs, fuzziness, digging holes, pulling weeds, picking green beans, making lunches for other people, witty banter, double entendres, things that are wee, out of date slang, iron chef of the mind, rain on aluminum roofs, days in the library, sweatshirts, prolonged eye contact, getting letters, trivia, chewing, being upside down, urban exploring, being quiet, laughing loudly, smiling at strangers, pushing buttons, swing sets, snow people, eyebrows, the many shades of brown, peeing outside, poking things with sticks, building from the ground up, overcast days, hats, bagpipes, accordions, a good bass line, tree lined streets, accents, the smell of things baking, weekly rituals, breaking out of your comfort zone, dancing, making up jokes, whittling, back rubbing, horrible tattoos, recycling, blue collar indignation, curry, leftover birthday cake, hucking stuff, making up words, reading poetry aloud, making people happy, high fiving, swearing, peace love and understanding, not mowing your lawn, wandering through aisles at the library or grocery store, peanut butter, sepia, onomatopoeia, the simplicity of it all, the complexity of everything, the idea of religion, the barter system, piglets, blanket nests, socialism, crappy coffee, hammocks, secret handshakes, riding in the back of a pickup truck, bare feet, farmers markets, giddiness, porches, plaid, pigtails, photosynthesis, letting things go

and burning bridges, forgiveness, brand new experiences, going to school, heavy lifting, rock climbing, sunrises, watching things happen, sore muscles, new socks, self-sufficiency, recognizing your influences, contradictions, hippos, spoonerisms, multi-tasking, sign language, sleeping bags, garlic, ska music, science fiction, sketching faces, old Playboys, capes, sticking your finger into something rotten, making horrible faces, light pollution, gratuitous use of quotation marks, thunder, putting cherry pits in my belly button, shock value, doing dishes, wearing slippers, making lists, late night excursions, working through problems, puns, Poe's Law, irony, interconnectedness, button up shirts, middle school humor, making mashups of the Sunday comics, sharing common experience, being overwhelmed by humanity, running and hiding, fragmented memory, time trials, opposable thumbs, using gum to pick my nose, science experiments, wrestling matches, micro fiction, surrealism, Martin van Buren, when my hair freezes, public showers, summersaults underwater, when my family's all together, kisses all over, coincidence, writing bONEr on $1 bills, wearing costumes, eye liner, wine in coffee mugs, discussing the newspaper, birds pecking between my toes, bats, meteor showers, nights on the roof, titties, random acts of kindness, seeing where the night takes you, thinking backward, someone else cutting my toenails, children's museums, Dr. Seuss, the idea of Vermont, lucid dreams, stoned Bingo, opening jars, cobblestones, anything that Brendan Small does, dirt and digging, using a bow saw, pigeon   pose, holding snakes, opiates, swimming into waves, tree houses, mentally transporting myself to the 1970's when all the rock stars look like they do on their album covers, shade, spirals, fractals, plaid, linguistics, emergence theory, de-eyeing potatoes, knives, sexual tension, snow forts, shoveling, setting things on fire, hilarious coffee mugs, poking at stuff, giving people rides on my bike, mangoes, contests, arm wrestling, opening music for 'As it Happens', historically accurate graphic novels, smiles, Laundromat solidarity, anticipating the next   song on an album, rainbows that come out right before the sun goes down, conspiracy theories, roundhouse kicks, the green power puff girl, dysphemisms, RadioLab, sidewalk chalk, jelly beans, clothespins, nerve endings, life – the cereal, board game, and state of consciousness, wagging tails, praying mantids, paul simon, sex advice columnists, knuckles, cankles, lined paper, Teenage Mutant Ninja Turtles - especially Michelangelo the party dude, restless leg syndrome, first world problems, bluegrass, MC Escher drawings and Rube Goldberg devices, boys in dresses, conversations about arm hair, Scotland!, falling asleep at the library, parents who love me, slang terms for vagina, touching my face with my feet, biting my shoulder, clean rooms, near death experiences, being invincible, mycology – the study of fungi, feti, poonfar – the highly illogical period that occurs every seven years when Vulcans mate, roommate solidarity, owl pellets, animal grunts, threatening to ride wombats, a sense of community, using wine and coffee for cooking, trading clothing, shorts and stocking caps, bending at the waist, hating people in my head, avoiding peanut butter falling from the grinder, stupid arguments, drawing on tattoos to fit the occasion, sitting on the floor at a bookstore, a stack of magazines, library websites, looking at people's google history, anthropomorphizing zits, mash ups between animals giving birth and cysts being drained, weight lifting, theatrically dragging my foot or limping, candle wax, clothespins, clotheslines, lips, licking, holding hands, 5 am, reading 3 books at once, airplane bathrooms, trains, Iceland, Irish wit, Balkan lit, Indian bucket showers, condiments, food processors, tempeh, bike tours, hammocks, mixtapes, mouthguards, soccer, shag carpet, petlessness, landing tricks, road rash, the moon walk, fuzzy nuzzles, freckles, bowling, derbin, unexpectedly catching something, crooked teeth, referencing Gremlins, creating a pretentious back story for something frivolous, forgiveness (because it bears repeating), and kindness (for the same reason)

Sit up, shut down

I've searched and researched for a perch on the tree of knowledge, a pocket in a shirt in the closet of understanding.

All I got is this seat on the short bus, a stupid grin on my face and two bucks in quarters I'll turn into wishes as I flip them in the fountain.

The sign says 'no swimming' but I write 'just kidding' underneath in magic marker. They call them magic because when you smell them you go to different planets. They call them markers cause some guy named Mark invented them, I bet. Caveman Mark with some charcoal and a heart of gold. As soon as I get ahold of a computer I'm going to make a Wikipedia page for him. Then I'll eat some dinner. The more you know, the merrier you'll be. The less you eat, the skinnier you'll seem. We make a good team, this magic marker and me. We go to infinity and back every evening. Infinity is the strip club my mom works at.

Evening is like odding only opposite. I think I'm a mix like a twist cone, vanilla chocolate. Oh! Now I'm all hot and bothered melting on the cement, looking for cracks in the sidewalk of enlightenment.

Balancing Act

In the middle of the road at high noon in the Old West
the men took measured steps and breathed deep and
died dusty deaths.

In the Middle of the East the women are fighting for
the right to bare arms and headscarves cover head scars
and cars drive themselves without license.

Caution thrown to the winds blows over boulders, rocks
and rivers, rolling stones. All directions. Broken home is
where the heart split like cord wood and splinters still
catch when they're least expected. The dead and the
almost dead held gently in the mind's eye of the
disbelievers. Dry eyes. Die trying. Circle of life. Rebirth.
Revolution. Turn turn turn.

For everything there is a reason even if it's not
reasonable. In every kingdom there is treason even if
it's not fruitful. Apple as metaphor and Eve as evil. Let
them eat cake. Let them burn at the stake. Let them
break themselves on the unscale-able walls and fall and
fall and fall until there is nothing and no one at all in the
middle.

Review of Graceland

Every song is like... what?! And the intros. And he says so much crazy shit. Empty like a pocket. Fuck. I think I'll cry.

Pocketship

Last night Paul Simon whispered in my ear about emptiness. Emptiness like pockets.

I met a man with no cigarettes. He was nothing but want. I met a man who wanted nothing but to walk back and forth, give away everything, piece by piece. He gave the other man a cigarette. I found a lighter in one of my pockets. I found a stone toad. Eight quarters that I never played pool with. Losing at pool is a hobby that I could drop in a heartbeat. Forget in an inhale.

Give up like a daughter for adoption. Never look back. Not looking. Closing my eyes, I was my own person.

Opening them up, I was everyone. I was white light and stars and the whole sky was my jello semen umbrella.

The cold pavement was my pillow. A hard pill to swallow. I kept it under my tongue and showed the night nurse my tonsils. When she moved on to morning I spit it in my coffee and poured the whole pot in my closet. The clutter was wet and confusing. Full as

My pockets. I am nothing but change. My eye sockets. I can do nothing but see.

My stomach. I can do nothing but eat. My lungs. I have become what I breathe. My head. Empty like a pocket.

Nothing but want but not wanting enough to be it.

Golden Arc

Apple tree, happy meal. The acorn doesn't fall far at all. The omelet uncooks itself, cools down. Yolks ooze into shells sewn shut. Up into chickens and the sun settles into the east. Takes heat with it. Cold dark apartment. A part of what I meant left when I said it. Never edit. Never mind. Blind eyes are hiding in plain sight. Deaf ears are right here. Numb fingers full of empty feeling look so lifelike from outer space. If things were as they seamed, these threads would never forget. The colors wouldn't run. Permanent sunset. Perpetual cat pets. Step children. Foot rests. I have a corgi for that. I have a couch that won't quit and a crown for each of my teeth. This floor is beneath me! Bring me something butter. With more butt! To hold down my couch! Cause the floor's so slippery! With butter! Even your mother thinks so!

Wicked Witch

I store all the worry in my forehead like a billboard,
collapsible suitcase. The face underneath gets forgotten
and matted down like grass under a picnic basket. I'm
full of delicious, I promise. I'm full of shit right up to
my brown eyes. I'm an apple you bite into with strong
teeth and you don't notice the worms as much as the
holes long after you've swallowed.

Infomercial

Over the course of a portion of the evening, perceptions were deceiving and my mind's eye led my inner child down a hallway with walls that seemed to be breathing, teeth and finger paintings of family portraits at random intervals. The overall feeling was one of being digested. Downright biblical. I was drowning in my own assumptions when the sky opened up and threw me a bone. I think it was my own because as soon as I grabbed hold, my leg fell off. And that's how I lost 10 pounds in 5 seconds. Now I don't feel embarrassed when I take my shirt off at the jim. Jim being the name of my dealer. Good guy. Nice smile.

Hard to understand with that lisp, though.

Crush

The power of Christ compels me to tell secrets to
strangers.

The strange thing is that I don't believe in Jesus.

The lord works in mysterious ways and the universe is
always changing.

May the force of gravity be with you when you feel
alone on the sidewalk.

May feelings walk beside you, always.
Never lose your empathy or the hard shell it hides
b ehind.

I wish you would melt in my mind instead of my
mouth. Out, out strange demon.

Do you want to hear a secret? I have a crush on orange
soda.

Flashback

Dreams: classic but contemporary. 3-D but black and white.

You wore khakis and glass slippers, had a light saber and a pager. Ate Captain Crunch while reading the dictionary. You had flowers in your hair and a handgun in your waistband. You were wasted on research chemicals and absinthe. Your pocket watch was stopped at the right time and the alarm on your cellphone wouldn't stop going off.

When we went to board the train, you took off with your jetpack. I ended up biking and beat you to Canada. You said the altitude

helped with your allergies but made your toe tingle. Just the big one. I paid you 8 dollars in quarters to ask an old lady for directions. She sang us a song and fed us watermelon. We had to run around naked in the rain to rinse off the juice. We both fell down on an anthill and they took us to their queen. "Feed her cherry pits and balls of lint" you whispered but I was empty belly buttoned. I scratched her head instead and she gave me three wishes. All of them were to be in bed with you, halfway asleep and kissing your shoulders. I woke up with sore lips and anthill sand in my hair.

Mermanatee

Sometimes I pull the trigger on my squirt gun like it's
going to bring forth the end of the world

and sometimes I bite my lip so hard I wonder if I'm not
part velociraptor

and sometimes I slam the door so jarringly I think my
head might fall off and roll down a hill and into a sea
filled with weeds and manatees cross-dressed as
mermaids

and sometimes I'm so self-conscious that I think all the
songs on the radio are about what I'm supposed to be
doing

and sometimes I drink my coffee so hot it blots out the
sun for a minute or two

and sometimes when I'm peeing in my yard I think
about you and what you're doing.

Chicago

- I made a list
- Of things
- I don't like and
  You
- Weren't
- On it

Pipe Dream

Sometimes the pipes that crawl under my sink and into the dirt sound like machine guns.

Sometimes like something the size of a house that purrs.

Sometimes, a movie star will be standing on a purple carpet, smiling. And I'll think,

the color on my television is off again. The rats in the walls sound like an audience that isn't paying attention. They're fighting in the aisles with teeth and whiskers and I wish I had a tail. Not like a rat but like a comet. Maybe I just wish I could fly. My window is on the second floor and I can fall and I can land but I'd never jump.

If I had a pair of chutes I'd slide down the right one and my identical twin would take the left. We'd fall out the bottom, onto the purple grass, like we were in a commercial for chewing gum.

Sometimes the pipes in my house sound like one room gnawing on another.

And swallowing.

And shitting out televisions.

Costumed

Flip myself inside out. My smile's not a frown, now, it's a big wet hole that I still sing songs through. The voice in my head is tone deaf, sounds like it wears braces, has a case of the 'I love you, I hate you, I love you's.'

Sometimes flower petals fall from my ears and I know she's at it again. Fuck or fight, fists, lips, kisses like kicks to the teeth. Love hurts like a burning case of church bells. Hell is a spelling bee in a different language. I'm allergic to religion and insects. I suspect it's all in my head but my doctor says I'm paranoid. My doctor is the internet. My only friend is the light above my neighbor's garage.

My head is a lemonade stand in a ghost town. When life gives you one of those, what choice do you have but to stick out your tongue, hit the road, change your clothes and your astrological sign? That's a club I would join. That's a dotted line I would sign if you held a gun to my head and handed me a pen.

If I keep saying yes than I'll keep getting stepped on. I don't trust gravity so I depend on the weight of other people's problems to keep me grounded. The dirt under my fingernails is a brand new universe. Curse this infection of knowledge. Feelings.

I'm a bowl full of cold spaghetti pretending to think.
I'm a dish of peeled grapes trying to see. My Halloween
costume is me. Is me inside out. Is me on the ground. Is
meat and bones and holes and a bunch of flower petals
falling toward the forest floor, not making a sound.

The Worst

Don't you hate it when, like, a waitress says "Enjoy your meal."

And you reply, "You too." And then you're like, *goddamn it I'm so stupid*, so you try to cover it up by saying "I'm sorry, I thought you were asking me what my favorite band was."

And it's killing you inside because you hate Bono which is only a little less than you hate The Edge but neither are as bad as Lars Urlich so when you realize you're still talking and saying

"Because it's a tie between them and Metallica," you're so full of self-loathing that you eat your food in angry bites and no, you don't 'enjoy your meal.'

Why would you enjoy anything when you're such a piece of shit clinging to existence like it was a shoe and you're still shit, in this scenario, just like every other one you can imagine for the rest of eternity. So you walk yourself to the closest bridge and jump off but of course you fuck up suicide like it was prom night and dying was the same as getting a date but instead you sat at home and watched I Love Lucy reruns which is what's playing in the hospital room when you come to and a nurse sees you wake up and you say,

"I really wish I'd died instead of breaking both legs." And she says, "Me too." And then she can tell she messed up so she goes "Meat, ewwww. I'm a vegetarian because I love animals so much."

And you say, "You know, Bono's a vegetarian as well. I know a lot of facts about him because he's in my favorite band, U2." And then you're like *whhhhhhhhhhhhhhhhhaaaaat's my problem?!?!?!?!*

Full House

One time this lady named Mary got knocked up and started a religion and another one had a little lamb and another one had a sister and they were twins and one time, when my family was driving, my brother called them Dirty Faced Kate and Stinky Olsen and my dad pulled over and said, "Do not make fun of the Olsen twins."

But this is about a different girl named Mary Tiedman who sang a song that told me not to trust a man with a first name for a last name.

I was like

Billy Joel… the piano man?

Bob Dylan… the tambourine man? Clark Kent… mother fuckin Superman?

And then I started thinking that it's really the last names that are trouble because John Wayne was okay until the Gacy part got added then he just started killing boys willy nilly dressed in a clown suit.

So maybe it's clowns that can't be trusted because that Ronald guy is giving everyone heart disease and his last name's pretty awesome. And he's like "Do you believe in magic?" And "Do you want fries with that?" and I'm all "I guess I'd take some magic fries if it's not too much trouble."

No trouble at all, apparently, because they appear in front of me and I'm looking for ketchup but Ronald reads my mind and goes "Sorry, this is a condiment free establishment." And I glance around and see that I'm surrounded by a lot of sad, stressed out people. Then Billy Joel starts playing on the radio. *We didn't start the fire. It was always burning since the world's been turning.* And, oh god, I realize that I'm in hell. And then, I guess Mary Tiedman was right.

But only for a second cause, duh, Paul Simon. So I say, "What about Paul Simon?"

And Ronald's all, "What about Rob Thomas?" And I remember this one time my brother was driving to L.A. for a Magic tournament and ended up behind a guy with a Matchbox 20 decal on the rear window of his pick-up and a MB20FAN personalized license plate.

Soooo, maybe that was hell?

But Mary Tiedman steps into the vestibule of my mind to set some things straight and says

1) This is just a regular McDonalds

2) There is no hell

3) I never meant for you to take my songs so seriously and

4) What's your dad's deal with the Olsen twins?

And I don't know so I just slip out the back, Jack. Make a new plan, Stan. Set myself free, Lee. And don't think twice, cause it's all right.

Meow

It's raining cats and dogs like Pavlov was ringing his bell and drool was spooling down from the heavens. Like the bell was thunder. Like it was birthed from lightning instead of running behind, still tying its shoes. Yelling.

Dogs hate thunder. Don't wear shoes. Dog spelled backwards is God.

Gods in Egypt were Jackals, Beetles, Cats. "God is dead." Nitzche

"Nitzche is dead." Physician

"Curiosity killed the cat." Someone's mother Shrodinger considers the cat in the box in his mind. Is it alive or dead? The man isn't sure. Isn't paying attention. He's watching the rain hit a window that he knows is melted sand. He's never been to beaches, tasted the ocean. Is he alive or dead?

Yes

teeth

I heard your dad dropped everything to become a dentist. I heard your mother left him. I hurt myself today. Johnny Cash was singing in the background. I crashed into something. I was cut open. I was chopping onions with closed eyes. I cried before and after but they meant different things. I burned dinner but you forgot to give me everything so I think we're even. I miss your father all the time. I bite the inside of my cheek and smile. I found your list of fears in a pile of laundry. I washed it and watched them disappear, disintegrate. I wish you were someone else. I think I'm late or early. Everyone I know goes away in the end.

But I think this is just the beginning. Just baby teeth.

Walking around the block, talking to my doctor about lockjaw and mocking the rockstars with their sock drawers all disarrayed

Life is juicy like a peach,
like bodies washed up on the beach,
like the Buddha swollen with teachings and
the police with their pepper spray poised to freeze
speech.
See the violins inherent in the system, playing beautiful
music to get tangled up in. Let your hair down,
give your shoes to someone.
Set fire to passions that will melt your skin off and mark
you for life.
Pull an Albert Hoffman and ride a bike. Make like a tree
and grow towards the light. Fight for your right to bite
down on the fruit that will set you up to lose
but chose to let that juice run down your chin and
into the ocean that will absorb you like loose change in
couch cushions.

Things you don't want to mistake for other things when putting in your mouth:

Milk for Orange Juice.
Water for Vodka.
Vodka for water.
Soap for cheese.
Olive oil for honey.
Little pieces of deodorant trapped in the carpet for popcorn.

Books about books about forgetting how to read

Seconds and centuries disappear into the same desk drawer as uranium and love letters and handguns halfcocked like beer soaked erections, entire families buried in landslides in third world countries I couldn't find on a map if you put a textbook to my head and told me to learn by osmosis. As if my brain were as porous as my conscience, propped up on excuses and hurt feelings and scar tissue that will fade because time heals all wounds and all's fair in love and more money means more problems that crawl under your bed while you're sleep walking

Where do you get your Umami?

There was a whole day where I was a do-nothing and it was full of holes and I filled them with tree branches and leaves and sand and rocks and the way the river moved on top of the sound of traffic.

And I thought - fuck those painters who make the landscapes that are put on the walls of hospitals where we go to watch people die and be born. Fuck them because we look at trees and a horizon and they seem like an oil painting and they sound like jazz music and that makes it ok to go about what we're doing which is nothing, usually, or driving.

I said, wouldn't it be horrible to tell someone, "I love you so much that I'd pay one hundred people to write I love you over and over for an entire day on paper made from trees like these."

And you said, "At least 100 people would get to think about love." And then my head exploded but when I put it back together I decided that it's a fallacy to believe that we're ever really thinking about what we're doing.

And I wondered if fallacies even apply to emotions and you said "No, they're an incorrect argumentation in reasoning resulting in a misconception or presumption."

And then I asked if you got sad during the winter. And you said, "I don't know but I get really happy in the spring time."

Which is wonderful - like paint running, like blood dripping, like a poem, like putting your feet in the river and not wishing you were anywhere else.

Intelligent Designer Sunglasses

like smiling makes you happy like practice makes you
perfect like plastic lives forever floating in the ocean
like fires burning forests, erosion melting mountains
like dinosaurs exploding and blastocysts dividing like
drowning in the moment and choking on your vomit
on roads that lead to nowhere with posies in your
pocket like plagues of locusts like second hand smoking
like 'let there be light-ing' like Big Brother is watching
like Kafka is morphing like the Kids are all Righting like
new beginnings like falling off the wagon like day light
savings and time's a wasting like muscle memory like
mob mentality like two plus two is five-ing like The Joy
of Cooking like all of history has brought you to this
moment where you're going to do exactly what you're
supposed to right … now.

Dirt

There once was a guy named Dirt, a salt of the earth fellow humble as a pie is round and quiet as the wing beats of the Tooth Fairy. He could tell stories about holes in the ground that made you feel like you were there among the roots and rocks and worm tunnels. Maybe he was speaking from experience. Maybe he just wasn't afraid of the dark the way that a lot of us are.

He had a voice for radio and a beat up Volvo that got 30 miles to the gallon. Dirt only looked at calendars for the pictures so he saved a lot of money when he bought them years later. A penny saved is more ballast for your pockets. This is why Dirt left deep foot prints that later filled with water and became lakes for the area insects. Dirt liked putting shells to his ear so he could imagine the ocean. He died from a spider bite with a smile on his face like he knew where he was going.

[Man]

The man looked at the pie resting on the table. It had crinkled edges that looked like a ring of crusted tongues circling the scene of an accident. The tongues were flaking off and getting tangled in the fiber of the table cloth. Maybe the tongues were more like fall leaves. Maybe the leaves were circling the accident.

The man's mind turned to the accident. He didn't remember any leaves, but then he didn't remember much beyond the thick strawberry syrup pouring out of his groin. The man hated women, he was a misogynist, so he refrained from comparing the clotted flow to that of menstrual blood, the inner lining of the uterus. *Uter this* he thought to himself and crushed a fly creeping along the corner of his own shiny table.

The man crushed the fly like he himself had been crushed physically and spiritually during the accident. He had Type O blood, the universal donor. The man's mother followed a diet called "The Eat for Your Blood Type Diet." The man thought that this was stupid.

Then again, if he'd been somewhere eating something for his blood type instead of where he'd been at that particular time, he wouldn't have been crushed so physically and spiritually. In fact, in another reality, a better one, he may have been sitting in this particular diner. Maybe he would have been enjoying a slice of strawberry pie, the filling of which he would not associate with his internal workings. Oh, the freedom in that thought! Anxious to make it a reality, he beckoned the waitress over.

She ambled up dutifully, trying not to stare at the scars. "I think I'd like a piece of that strawberry pie," the man spoke with a voice that sounded like the assured ticking of all the Republican boxes on the voter's ballot.

"Oh, I'm sorry sir," the waitress angled her voice upward to indicate apology, "What you're lookin' at there is our rhubarb pie." The man gazed at her a moment as if he were stoically passing a kidney stone then he put his face in his hands and sobbed and sobbed.

Eggplant

I don't sleep so well anymore, the skin under my eyes purples out like a cliché, like eggplants. Sunken down like plaster casts of thumbprints. Indents in bed sheets and blankets, a moonscape where the monotony is broken only by books marked by corner folds.

My room is a satellite where all the lights are reflections, time is relative but I always need to see what my watch says. For perspective. Music is piped in from overthere on tether cords like eggplant vines, sounds tracked by Sublime - sleeping by yourself at night can make you feel alone…

It's like all the good things happen by chance and we screw it up by over thinking. Or understanding. Maybe it's because you're on acid. Or religion. I blame it on mythology and the moon and the way that raindrops hit my window.

Sometimes I pee outside for perspective. Sometimes I go all day without talking. I have big, eggplant bruises on my thighs from watching the sky when I should be riding my bicycle. Maybe that's a metaphor for everything. But how can you learn if you don't fall?

My birth certificate is twenty-four years old. Like the music, it's irrelevant. I'm just cells and influence and empty spaces. I soak up the atmosphere like photosynthesis, like something cooked in olive oil and offered up like a handshake. I space on what day it is but like to know what my wrist says.

Hannah

Hannah is a palindrome
Is ambidextrous
Is bisexual
When I rip her in half
She looks in the mirror
And feels whole again
When she's gone
She leaves a hole
Blood sloshes over the lip
Of the rip
In the imperfect container
Of my heart
Together we're art
Apart we're saran wrap
Held taut by fingers
Someone flicks a lighter
And the world puckers
Gets darker
The smell of burned plastic
Coats my hair
And I wear her absence
Like a clay bowl full of cold water
The thing about me is that I always drop things
The thing about her is that she's afraid of falling
Sometimes Hannah is just
A hand to hold
A hammock to lie in
But sometimes she's a small bird

Ripped open by the side of the road
So violently
It makes you wonder
How the Fuck did that happen?
My greatest fears
Are running over a ground squirrel with my bike
And loving someone
Too hard.

Case of the Mondays

It takes a whole bunch of muscles to hang upside down from the shower rod in your bathroom trying to catch a glimpse in the mirror of your lips curling upward.

But what's the alternative? Smiling? Fuck that facial expression and the horse it rode in on. Like my head was a stable or the window on an airplane, transparent and changing daily. A buffet of meats arranged neatly according to the chemistry experiments in my head. I am not an open book. I am the bookshelf in front of a

stairway in Amsterdam. I have secrets that have climbed up inside me and will remain like stains on the walls long after the Gestapo does their house cleaning. If you ask me how I am I'll say swell like a can with botulism. I'm happy like the cow turned into a meal at McDonalds. Billions and billions of disturbed microbes pace my intestines like the words to Christmas carols sung in forgotten languages. I walk all night with my eyes closed and put out cigars on my arms to stay focused. I'm a machine in shitty packaging. I'm somebody's mother.

Case of the Wednesdays

I gather smiles from reflections in troubled water, plant them on the banks and watch trees grow twisted but brave across the void so that I may walk without distress to the other side. The grass here may not be greener but grows just as shyly toward the sky's bright bit of existence. Beauty is nothing but ideas we've stitched together and propped up in a spotlight that's hot and distracting. I like to live down and out of those hills in the hollows where mud floods the space between my toes and when I laugh it echoes and the shadows make it easy to shed fashion like reptilian skin and the mirrors are replaced with windows to each other's insides so we can find that we're all just a bunch of systems made of organs made of cells made of star stuff that flows through everything equally always.

Numb

Dear Marx,

   Given the choice I think I'll just take these opiates and leave the masses to their masses, the bells and whistles to the marching band, the lint from my dryer to the birds so they can make flammable nests then rise from the ashes like life was a Harry Potter movie. I'll take this seat in the theater and lean back in the dark like the world was my oyster and life has given me lemons as garnish. Every cloud with a silver lining like a stained glass window. Every one of my dreams set to go over like a lead zeppelin. All of the plants in my garden deep rooted like my convictions. Rap sheet a mile long like I was Public Enemy. Morale still higher than Snoop Dog in a limousine. Everything making sense like sine, cosine, tangents I tend to go off on like I was Robert Frost taking the road less traveled.

   Positioning the knights near my chess board like I'm ready for battle. They can watch me play checkers. I prefer to see the world in red and black as in, they read me my rights when I was blacked out so I don't think it counts. You should make like me and forget this all happened. Make like a bee, like Mohammad Ali, and settle this with violence. Maybe die in the process.

   That's not a threat, that's a promise, officer. But I was crossing my fingers. I know it's hard to tell when I'm joking cause I've got this great poker face, this straight laced haircut, knuckle tattoos that spell 'I love you' with a little rearrangement. I'm the Mr. Potato head of assumed identities but you can call me whatever you want. As long as it's not late to dinner. As long as the name on the prescription bottle matches the one I answer to.   I know I know I know I'm dead on the inside. I'm deaf, dumb, and blind to the idea that anyone could understand what I want out of life.

Blues

I've got those hit by a train blues and blacks and purples
I've got these come full circle walk a straight line issues
I've got concussions blooming like weeds in ditches I've
got left by the side of the highway sighs of contentment
Mingling with exhaust fumes
And burning holes through the ozone layer Like my
soul was escaping
Like it could ever get high enough

I've got these borrowed blues Like I'm old news
Like I'm left at the altar, burned at the stake, swallowed
whole by my mistakes
Like I'm a pair of shoes that someone walked A million
miles in
Now my soul's disconnected Slaps the pavement
Syncopates like heartbeats of children Smoking
cigarettes in doorways

I've got these red, white, and blues
This two party system split brain freeze dry mouth
symptom
This amber wave of grain belt beer belly up economy
This melting pot turned up real hot dog eat dog days of
summer lovin', leavin', hustle, and jivin'
This nothing new under the sun block buster hit and
runny nose nothing but talks a lot reputation
This 30 year locust, extended adolescence, bury me

backward, dessert for breakfast decadence.
These rotten teeth, these tired feet, this anxiety attack.

I've got these little boy blues Like I'm a fairy tale
Like I'm invincible
Like the sun could never hurt me Like we have an
understanding Like I put on my wax wings
And hum Stairway to Heaven Until someone yells Free
Bird Then I smell something burning

I've got these summertime blues
This red hot ready or not farmer's tan
This sand from my hour glass trickling into my swimsuit
I'm melting like an ice cube. Ocean salty like God's tear
drops
I drip like a Popsicle in a pressure cooker, a hooker in
church,
A beer can perched in a broken refrigerator.

But what I keep telling myself? Is that I've got you, babe
And you've got air conditioning.

Mirage

He's all 'If you were me.'
and sometimes she's like 'Maybe I am.'

She's peanut butter garlic and he's avocado jam and
yum. Yum.
Lips and tongue.

He's more man but not Morman at least not any more
man and she's lady like. Or girl ish. Or woman y. But
kind of hairy. At least everyone says so. At least in her
head when she's thinking about it. But she doesn't,
mostly.

He's mostly buried in sandcastles. Moats around his
toes where whole worlds exist and disappear. Take
nothing but footprints, leave salt water tears.
She's not a drop in the ocean, she's the entire ocean in
one drop. And he dropped out of school. And she's
always dropping things. And tripping over others.

When they trip together it's all colors.
He's brown and she's blue when they're reflected in
each other.

All alone he quietly rhymed with purple and she read

books in the green grass.

He's scratchy callouses and she's slippery no goodbye
but trying harder.

Vinegar and liquor like the taste of erasers in one ear
and out the other.

He's smart and she's glasses. He's art and she's crayons.
She's candy and he's a blue tongue.

She's half full, he's half full. Together they're a glass
with a hole, always filling each other.

He's not not asleep. She's not not awake. Same
opposite.

She's Medusa and he's stoned and she's drunk and he
has snakes in his hair or up his sleeve or he's Adam and
she's evolving. And both climb the branches of the
tree of knowledge.

He's four wheels and she's two left feet and they're
both the heat rising from the pavement.

She jumps. He's like, 'no, jump this way.' He jumps.
They're both 'ouch.'

He's a ball of hair and she's a rope ladder.
He's little cat feet in the fog in the city and she's sitting
in the sun squinting at the cornfields.

She feels feelings at least 60 percent of the time.

He kills time but not hamsters.

She would never do that on purpose.

He would like to propose toast. Or popcorn. Flavored bubble gum.

He's the crumbs from something and she eats deodorant off the carpet.

He's steeped in sisters like a sweet tea of estrogen and she's got more hands than family and drinks coffee like it was her job.

If she were a coffee taster she'd never sleep. If he were a court reporter he'd just repeat everything with his fingers.

Let's not do that, she thought to him. Ok, he thought back.

So they did something completely different and the world split open and flipped inside out and it looked the same but more shiny somehow.

But maybe they were the only ones who noticed.

The Beginning

Like This

She was singing. I was a song.

She turned left and I was wrong.

We tried to write each other with our eyes from across the room but it was smoky and I was too tired, like a bicycle.

She was asleep in the backseat while her parents argued their way across the Rocky Mountains.

I was a fountain pen drawing lines on a napkin. She was the horizon.

I was the sky.

She lied to me about hiding from something and I was a book left open on the bedside table for a week while the owner went on vacation and now my spine is all twisted.

She's a closet chiropractor. I'm a Velociraptor.

She was 9 years old when she saw Jurassic Park in the theater and I think that's the perfect age.

I'm fine wine and she's cheap whiskey. Together we're a parable from the Bible.

And drunk! We are so drunk.

And we are calling each other. And we are wrong numbers. She's tattoos and I'm barbed wire. She's the Holocaust.

I'm 300 pounds.

She's 50 euros.

I'm 5 dollars. She's a ginger.

That means red hair, not something you'd find in the grocery store.

We met in a grocery store. I wasn't lonely but she was lonely. I was content to be buying cereal by myself and then she wouldn't stop talking to me. She's still talking. I'm sleeping next to the phone and an open window with her name and number inked across my forehead. She's allergic to peanuts.

I'm indifferent. She's the president.

I vote in a church that's four or five blocks from my house.

I think that's a safe distance for a church to be but she said she'll have it moved if I ever burst open in stigmata.

She's a virgin like Mary and I'm a whore like Mary.

I'd like to get married but she's already married to like fifteen people,

I think she met them on the internet. She's a high speed modem and

I'm a pencil with a chewed off eraser.

She's a Taser and I'm protesting the deforestation of Sequoias in the Red Wood Forest. I've never been to California and she's so tan I think she fake tans, did you know that causes cancer?

She'll never stop growing.

I'm pocket-sized

and shrinking until it's like I don't exist

beyond the words and the melody of the song she's singing.

The Me is Silent

I don't know how to pronounce my last name. It's
something vaguely ethnic with too many consonants.
People either avoid saying it or sound it out slowly and
ask 'is that right?' I always say yes and adapt accordingly.
I try to embody the person who would have that name.
I can be professional or shifty or flirtatious or all at
once. I have a trunk full of clothes to change into. My
car is nondescript. There is nothing on my walls at
home but my cupboards are full of personality.
Sometimes that personality is mine. When I wake up, I
always know *where* I am because there's a big sign
that says 'you are here' that I've taped to the ceiling
above my sleeping bag. I often don't know

who I am, though, until someone tells me. The *why*
and *what* usually fall into place once I have the

who sorted. To figure out the *when*, I look at my
watch. The *how* I learned early on – When a man and
a woman love each other very much…

Exit Central

Sometimes I wonder if I'm the sweatiest I've ever been but then I'm like, Nahhhh, cause what if it happened when I was swimming and I just didn't realize it at the time or it was when I was a baby and my parents left me in the hot car with the windows closed while they were in the hardware store looking at paint for the patio furniture?

And sometimes I think maybe I'm the only person who's been in a certain place but then I see all the footprints and think, well maybe that's just a conspiracy and God put them there to let me know I'm not alone in the world but then I'm like, shut up brain. But sometimes, because I'm dyslexic, I say "Shut up, Brian" and I say it out loud and my brother, Brian, hears me and he punches me in the neck. And then I realize that I can't be the only person who's been here cause Brian was with me all along and we're in the paint aisle at

Wal-mart. And then Brian goes, "come on, tard," and we go look for our parents who are trying to find the perfect shade of green to make them forget their problems.

And sometimes I'm trying to choose between using the bread that I scraped mold off of to make a sandwich or just licking peanut butter off the spoon and then mom comes in and yells cause I'm allergic to peanut butter and I could die and maybe then she'd get some peace and quiet but I shouldn't do it anyway. And I say, 'I forgot.' And she says 'I'll give you something to forget' and punches me in the neck.

And sometimes I'm in the living room, watching the

paint dry on the baseboards, and I get dizzy and have a dream where I'm flying and I wonder if this is the way I dissociate from a life that I can't change and if we're all distracting ourselves from the reality that it will end and whatever we use to fill the space in between doesn't matter because we're dead anyway and these blue green walls will outlive us all.

2084

You don't have to expect the unexpected as long as you
accept it. Boy or girl or both as long as it has fingers and
toes or flippers and fins or fur on its skin or a good coat
of paint or strong branches or a tree swing or decent
gas mileage or a crossword puzzle half done on the
table at the homeless shelter or one last sip in that cup
of coffee or ten good people in the whole city or a
whole city of shit filled streets and wild dogs and iron
fisted dystopia with one candle burning in a secret
room, one book being read, one person not worrying.

Mic Check

Is this thing on or yawning or awful or full of lies or
lying down or down and out or out and in or inedible
or incredible or just pretty to look at? Sometimes art is
gum on the sidewalk. Sometimes you get stuck to a
thought that you can't escape from. Sometimes the
thought grows arms and legs and eyes and ideas and a
smile with a beard under it. Sometimes you fall in love
and sometimes it falls on you. Sometimes you call the
shots and sometimes you get shot from a canon, I mean
like a camera, like take a picture, it'll last longer but it
will taste even stronger if it's a song you sing to yourself
in the shower, I mean like meteors, like deep space
confetti God might have at her birthday party. I turned
forever today. I ate so much cake. There were so many
candles like a lake of fire and I blew til I blue til I
passed out. I turned around like a record and you were
there like a shadow, like an echo, like a picture I drew
1,000 words ago and the words were all YOU.

This time with frosting

I crossed my X's. Dotted my I's with hearts still beating. Tic tac tip toeing through kitchens, leaving all the ovens on. I baked you this cake. Burned your house down. Didn't stick around long enough to taste the ashes because I believe in leaving.

I think?

But could be okay with staying. Maybe?

It's the kind of thing that becomes true when you don't move. And then that's you, there. Armchair swallowing you like medication for the headache you've become unless you keep running but that doesn't mean it has to be away from something. What stays the same could be the wind in your hair and the nametag pinned to your fingerprints and the places you leave them.

Stay in touch. Feel things. Believe in people.

Constant motion is the same thing as living. Spinning spinning -make your own gravity, a cocoon you can break out of, clothes you wear and give to others to cover their own hurts and hopes and remember you by. I made you this pie. I cleaned your kitchen. I turned the lights off when I left and the note on your fridge is filled with nothing but well wishes written in wet ink so the U's and I's are always evolving.

Plaid

I don't know many lumberjacks. Scratch that. I don't
know any lumberjacks. That's ok. I've climbed enough
trees, sawed enough logs, worn enough plaid that I can
pretend I've walked a kilometer in their steel toed boots,
tripping on roots because I'm doing it blindfolded.

I don't know why that is, just how I imagine it. The
imagination is a dangerous thing. Sometimes it's the
best thing. I just read that hugs release oxytocin, make
you feel better about the world, connect you to the big
family portrait of humanity. Seeing the forest instead of
the trees. Seeing the leaves instead of the branches.

The further apart two things are, the better they look
together – a lumberjack and a princess walked into a bar
mitzvah. The lumberjack bumped into the doorframe
because she was blindfolded. The princess stuffed a
bunch of hors d'oeuvres into her corset. "So we can
have a picnic later," she stage whispered.

Because she was not a tree falling in the forest,
everyone heard her. It takes so many muscles to frown
you might as well get a medal for attempting it. The
effort expended in the room all of a sudden was
Herculean.

Then the gravity machine flipped off and everyone spun
upside down, taking their frowns with them. The
lumberjack took off her blindfold at that moment.

Look at all these smiles, she thought. Isn't life wonderful? And that's when the hugging began, like so many olive trees reaching their branches toward each other.

Umbrella

I bow down to the foresight involved in bringing an umbrella when it isn't even raining, locking the door on your way out, and knowing what you want to be when you grow up. I want to be a success story, a nobody, the part of an omelet that still believes it can fly. A foul ball that gets lost in the stands and found by the janitor's son. An impossible equation. The dirt that gets thrown over a landmine. A window that's nailed shut and surrounded by razor wire. A bedtime story. The back pocket in a pair of pants that are traveling the country. Any country. Except the one I'm in right now. I want to be an impacted colon and the sense of release from bungee jumping. I want to be the yawn that jumps from person to person. I want to be a relic on Antiques Roadshow. I want to be a bunny rabbit. I want to be obsolete like the channel changer on a television. I want to be a wave and a particle. I want to be the Appalachian Trail. I want to be a cannibal and a cannonball from the First World War and a camera around the neck of someone who thinks too much and talks too little. I want to be something that the pot calls the kettle. I will never go back. I will not surrender. I want to be Anonymous and collect all the royalty checks and start a coke habit. I want to stare at the sun while humming Stairway to Heaven. I want to be a room where good things happen. I want to be a telephone number that's remembered because it corresponds to certain letters. 244-848-8437. Try and guess that one. I'm an enigma. I'm worm food. I'm melting.

To my future love

I love how you always have a first aid kit in your Tahoe.
I love how you pretend it doesn't hurt when you get
your hair cut.

I love when your fingers are greasy from KFC and you
tickle me.

I love how you take the time to clean your guns.

I love how people wanted you to sell out but you stayed
real.

I love how you still have all your baby teeth in a satchel.
I love how one oversized testicle doesn't stop you from
sitting up straight.

I love how you shake off after a bath like the dog
Beethoven from the movie of the same name.

I love how you cried so hard during Beethoven (the
movie) that you herniated and now one ball is way
bigger.

I love how you eat lean meats and whole grains and are
committed to a healthy lifestyle.

I love how you get wasted on $1 beer night and call me
and yell.

I love how you buy things from Sky Mall for the pet
that we might get together.

I like that cheese tour we took one time.

I love lamp.

Orphan Andy

You can pick your friends and you can pick your nose but you can never come home again. That might as well be a plaque on the wall or highlighted in the Bible that a sad man hands me at the bus station. I could ask for directions but the fact is it doesn't matter where I'm going, the way that my shoes are pointing is just fine thanks. I look down to see where that is and it's hard to distinguish North from nowhere from a hole in the ground that leads all the way to China where a girl is mumbling. *This won't hurt a bit,* her lips seem to be saying but I think that she's daydreaming and I'm no mind reader but she's probably just singing along to the songs the fill the air around her headspace, pissing away time while her shoe soles erode like mountaintops or lollipops left in the rain on a sidewalk.

The Moral

Life: A Love Story

In which the protagonist slides through life, looking at faces that seem to be made of the same parts but mean different things. Lips and Their Uses: A Brief Overview.

In which the protagonist goes through phases of stifling sneezes. Bodily Functions and the Etiquette Surrounding Them: A Flow Chart.

In which the protagonist dies in a predictable way and, one million years later, the Earth is overrun with spider hamster hybrids. Life: A love story.

Masterpiece

If you give a million monkeys
A million typewriters
A million years later
They'll all be dead

Truth from the Buddha

If you are kind…
You will sleep easily
You will wake easily
You will have pleasant dreams
People will love you
Spirits and animals will love you
You will be protected by the Universe
External dangers will not harm you
Your mind will be serene
Your face will be radiant
You will die unconfused
You will be reborn in happy realms

About the Author

Sometimes, when I'm not thinking, I think it's the future or 5th grade when I was the last kid to stop wearing sweatpants and I got a standing ovation when I finally wore jeans or the other morning when I was wandering around my yard without glasses, waiting for the neighbors to pull out of their driveway so I could pee beside the house or an alternate universe where I died in a train wreck or I'm inside the head of everyone throughout history who's ever chopped mushrooms while looking out the window or I'm one of the rats that's always chittering around in my walls. But then I'm like naaahhh, it's Now! And now. And now. And I must be me.